ITALIAN AND ROMAN FEASTS

Welcome to Roma

This cookery book is a modern interpretation of Ancient Roman repasts, a fusion of Roman and Italian cuisine transported from the Roman *culina* into today's Italian kitchen; but maintaining the history and integrity of the original Classical recipes. They are inspired by the gastronome and *bon viveur* Marcus Apicius, who lived, cooked and entertained during the reign of Emperor Tiberius in Imperial Rome some 2,000 years ago. He was, by all accounts, the Antonio Carluccio of his time. Over 450 of his recipes were recovered and translated in the aftermath of the decline of the Roman Empire, *circa* 350 AD, and these form the foundation of this book, brought up to date into the Italian kitchen.

The dishes are simple, imaginative and colourful – Italian modern-day food with a Classical twist.

A cornucopia of piscean platters, chicken and duck, veal, venison, pork and beef, the menus are accompanied with double sauces and explosions of fresh herbs and spices and a wide range of recipes prepared with the best of Italian vegetables, pulses, salads and sun-blessed fruit.

Each recipe is heralded with an English, Italian and Latin title.

ABOUT THE AUTHOR

Gilly Hall Travers began her academic career studying Latin and Ancient Greek at Royal Holloway and Bedford College at the University of London where she discovered a lust for Italian and Roman Cuisine.

She then took herself down a different avenue in life, balancing designer budgets and fashion shows with such aspiring talent as Jasper Conran and Georgina Godley.

Gilly's next journey took her to BBC Radio Oxford where she managed the station's Financial and Personnel status and produced the Children in Need Events.

Oh and she found herself a husband, Mark Travers, the Engineer in Chief.

The following step was to begin a new career amidst the laurels of the BBC again, at Television Centre in Shepherds Bush working with the Controller of BBC One's Channel team, Alan Yentob, as a Financial Manager. BBC One then took a turn to reorganize BBC Daytime and Gilly became Business Manager.

Gilly was then invited by Jane Lush, Head of BBC Daytime, to join the Entertainment team where she commissioned a steady stream of programmes with Jane's full support: *Dale's Wedding* (the blessed Dale Winton). The *Three Men in a Boat* series with Griff Rhys Jones, Dara Ó Briain and Rory McGrath hit the silver screen. She was Commissioning Editor for *Masterchef*, with John Torode and Greg Wallace; *Have I Got News for You*, with Jimmy Mulville, esteemed proprietor of Hattrick Productions, with Ian Hislop and Paul Merton; *Would I Lie to You?* with Rob Brydon, David Mitchell and Lee Mack.

She also worked on a different palette of quizzes such as *School's Out*, *Only Connect*, *University Challenge*, *Mastermind* and *A Question of Sport*, all of which made a footprint on BBC's Entertainment canvas and the annals of television, and many entertaining documentaries with Sir David Frost, Neil Morrissey and Penelope Keith.

Gilly Hall Travers

ITALIAN AND ROMAN FEASTS

AUSTIN MACAULEY PUBLISHERS™

LONDON * CAMBRIDGE * NEW YORK * SHARJAH

First Published (2018)
Austin Macauley Publishers™ Ltd.
25 Canada Square
Canary Wharf
London
E14 5LQ

DEDICATION

To my boys Mark and Marcus

ACKNOWLEDGEMENTS

To my husband Mark and our son Marcus
for being mostly happy to be subjected to my daily stream of lunches and suppers Also to
my Dinner Party victims in the village of Chearsley, Buckinghamshire

To Jane Lush for her support
To Sharon Sampson for her delightful photographs www.sharonsampson.co.uk
To Alicia Howard for her stunning illustrations alicia@allaboutartwork.uk
To Monika Kaliszuk for her excellent Italian Translation
To Tara 'Lady T' for her appreciation of my Piscean Dishes
To Jamie and Tina Cadle for their culinary advice
To my family, Judy, Louis and Janet for their support

And not forgetting my cousins, Ali, Alex, Julian, Peter,
James, Linda, Jenna, Ashley and Uncle Dennis
for their enthusiastic Christmas appetites

To Bob and Ida for their equally lovely support
Aunty Eva for her Praline Cake – always a hit
And to Princess Anna for helping me with my manuscript
And on the back page,

*"Best wishes from Gilly, Mark and Marcus
and we hope you enjoy the Show"*

RECIPES

CHAPTER THREE
MAIN COURSE MEAT AND GAME

CHAPTER FOUR
PISCEAN FISH DISHES

CHAPTER FIVE
LA DOLCE VITA

CHAPTER SIX
THE LIBATIONS

CHAPTER ONE
Super Soups and Starters

GREENER THAN GREEN GARDEN SOUP

The Ingredients

A generous handful of spinach

An equally generous handful of parsley

Celery leaves

Three ounces of garden peas

Two ounces of butter

A pint of vegetable stock

Ten grindings of pepper

A little sea salt

Slivers of Parmesan

A tablespoon of yogurt

Preparation Time 10 minutes
Cooking Time 30 minutes
Serves 4

The Italians love their vegetables which are plentiful in such a warm climate and with a fair sprinkling of rainfall, particularly in northern Italy. They aid digestion and a healthy stomach.

In Classical times the Romans called this pottage a "verdant gustatio", your green starter for 4.

Place the spinach, parsley, celery leaves and peas in a pan and gently sauté in butter for 10 minutes. Retain a little parsley to adorn the soup when about to serve. Then add the salt and pepper and the pint of vegetable stock and simmer for half an hour on a moderate heat. Leave to cool and then whizz up with a whisk or blender. You may wish to adjust your seasoning.

The humble pea is the star in this soup – adding a brightly green colour and a little texture.

Warm up and serve your garden soup atop with the slivers of Parmesan, a swirl of yogurt and sprinkle with parsley.

CUM GRANO SALIS
With a grain of salt
Salt was part of the salary of Roman cohorts. Hence the phrase.

VALENTINE'S ASPARAGUS CREAM SOUP WITH PARMESAN CROUTONS

The Ingredients

100 Grams of asparagus tips

One pint of chicken stock

Sea salt and black pepper

A few tablespoons of grated Parmesan

Bread cubes for the Parmesan croutons

A vanilla pod

Olive oil

Sunflower oil

3 Tablespoons of double cream

Chives and mint for decoration

Preparation time: 5 minutes
Cooking time: 30 minutes
Serves 4 for a starter

Asparagi Zuppa di Crema con Crostini Parmigiano Valentina

*

ASPARAGUS VALENTINO CREMOR PULMENTI ET PARMESAN

So, to begin, heat up the chicken stock and add the asparagus, sea salt, pepper and the vanilla pod, then cook gently for 30 minutes – no longer as asparagus is a delicate vegetable. Whilst your good pottage is cooking, make the Parmesan croutons. Cut up some cubes of bread and dip in olive oil and dust with the grated Parmesan.

Then heat up the sunflower oil and immerse the croutons for about 3 minutes on a medium heat so they are nice and crispy.

Whilst you are cooking these, whizz up the soup in a blender and blitz until velvety in consistency, then add the double cream, keeping a little for a kingly swirl on top.

Serve up with the cream and Parmesan croutons and decorate with chives and mint.

OMNIA VINCIT AMOR
Love conquers all

MARCUS'S MARVELLOUS MUSHROOM SOUP

The Ingredients

Half a pound of mushrooms
(I used chestnut mushrooms as
they have a lovely nutty flavour)

One ounce of butter

A quarter pint of chicken stock

One dessertspoon of black onion seeds

Half a leek grated

Half a pint of white wine

A generous handful of fresh green coriander

Three tablespoons of double or clotted cream (and keep a tablespoon for the celebratory swirl when plating up)

A grating of lemon zest, salt and pepper

Preparation Time: 5 minutes
Cooking Time: 30 minutes
Serves: 4 Hungry guests for a starter

Zuppa di Funghi di Marcus

*

MIRABILIA MARCUS IUS FUNGORUM

Sauté the mushrooms in the butter with salt and pepper for 5 minutes on a low heat and then add the black onion seeds. Then include the grated leek and lemon zest and half of the fresh, green coriander and simmer for a further minute.

Add the chicken stock for 5 minutes and then the white wine for 15 minutes. Stir in 3 tablespoons of cream and watch and wait simmering gently for a further 5 minutes.

When cooled up whisk up in a blender.

Warm the soup and plate up in bowls with an imperial swirl of cream and a flourish of coriander.

This is a diminutive gustatio/little starter, tickling the palette before the main course. The nutty flavour of the mushrooms is balanced with the bite of the black onion seeds and the complement of the cream.

ARS AMANDI
The art of love

LUSCIOUS LETTUCE SOUP

The Ingredients

Lettuce – lollo rosso, cos or round

A few blades of shallots

One tablespoon of chives and coriander

A dessertspoon of fennel leaf

Two dessertspoons of olive oil

Sea salt and pepper

Half a pint of chicken stock

Half a pint of goat's milk –creamier than cow's milk

But if you run out of goat's milk, cow's milk will be fine

Two dessertspoons of crème fraîche

Parsley fronds to finish

Preparation Time: 5 minutes
Cooking Time: 35 minutes
Serves: 4

Zuppa di Lattuga

*

IUS LACTUCAE

Heat the olive oil and sauté the shallots for a minute on a gentle heat so that they turn a pale yellow.

Add the chives and coriander and melt for a further minute.

Meanwhile, wash your lettuce head and chop up and add to the oil and herbs. Further baptise with the chicken stock, add the salt and pepper and fennel leaf. Simmer for 25 minutes on a low heat.

Then pour the soup into a blender and whisk for a few minutes. Add the goat's milk and heat gently for 10 minutes, grinding in a few more rounds of pepper.

Serve with some crème fraîche atop and dress with the parsley.

This is a very subtle soup but substantial. Delicate in flavour and it has a beauteous, mossy green colour. It is even better if you cook it the day before and let it soundly infuse.

The soup is best served with some fresh bread and a chilled glass of white wine.

DA MIHI SIS POCULUM VINI ALBI
I'll have a glass of white wine

BROAD BEAN SOUP WITH SHRIMPS AND A TRIFLING TRUFFLE OIL

The Ingredients

Two pounds of shelled fresh or frozen broad beans

Two ounces of butter

A pint of chicken stock

Two generous tablespoons of brown shrimps

Two black truffles

Two tablespoons of olive oil

One clove of garlic

A handful of fresh mint

A few strands of sage

Seal salt and pepper

Double cream for a princely swirl

Preparation Time: 10 minutes
Cooking Time: 40 minutes
Serves: 4 for a starter

Zuppa di Fagioli con Gamberetti et un Olio al tartufo

*

FABA CUM PISCE ET CUM TUBA OLEUM

Melt the butter over a low heat and add and coat the broad beans for 5 minutes. Then pour in the chicken stock and the fresh mint – you can use mint sauce if you don't have fresh mint to hand.

Improvisation is liberating.

Also add sea salt and pepper.

Simmer for 30 minutes and then whizz up in a blender.

Whilst this is simmering, sauté the crushed garlic with the shrimps.

Then do the same with the truffles and olive oil for just a few minutes.

Plate up the soup in bowls with the garlicky shrimps and a swirl of cream with the shredded sage on top.

Serve the truffle oil aside and some dippy chunks of bread.

DE RERUM NATURA
The Nature of Things

Taken from a poem by Lucretius, first century BC writer, describing the science of the universe and another first step forward in philosophy offering the thought that nature can work without the supernatural gods' influence.

PARSNIP, APPLE AND PEAR SOUP WITH SAGE LEAVES

The Ingredients

Two parsnips

One apple

A nice pear

Two ounces of butter

A quarter of a pint of double cream or clotted cream, keeping some aside for a swirl on top

Half a pint of chicken stock

Freshly shredded sage leaves

Sea salt and pepper

Preparation Time: 15 minutes
Cooking Time: 40 minutes
Serves: 4 for a starter

Pastinaca Mela e Pera Zuppa

*

PASTINACA CUM MALUM ET PIRUM SALVIA

Prepare the parsnips, apple and pear by removing the skins. Warm up the butter and immerse them all in the golden liquid for 10 minutes on a low and subtle heat so that they turn happily pale.

Heat up the chicken stock with the sea salt, pepper and the cream.

Simmer the parsnip and fruits in the stock for 30 minutes and then whisk up in a blender. If you don't have one then just give the mixture a masterful sieve.

When nice and crumbly return to the pan and add a little more cream for a further 10 minutes.

When you are satisfied and happy with the consistency and flavour, serve up with the shredded sage and a dash of dreamboat cream on top.

OMNE TRINUM EST PERFECTUM
Everything in threes is perfect

This adage is reflective of the ancient belief in holy magic: the Three Graces, the Three Muses, the Trinity and 'We Three Kings of Orient Are'.

ALMOND SOUP WITH GARLIC AND FAVA BEANS

The Ingredients

Four ounces of crushed almonds

One shallot sliced up

One clove of garlic

A little butter

Half a pint of chicken stock

A quarter a pint of single cream

Two ounces of fava beans, or butter beans if that is easier to find

Keep back a few beans to float on top with the watercress

Sea salt and black pepper

Watercress to decorate

Preparation Time: 10 minutes
Cooking Time: 20 minutes
Serves: 4

To begin …

Heat up the butter gently and immerse the sliced shallot and garlic. Cook for 5 minutes and then add the crushed almonds for a further few minutes.

After that prep stir in the chicken stock and the beans, salt and pepper. Again for a further 15 minutes.

Then waltz up in a blender and add the cream.

Warm and serve up with the remaining beans and the watercress sprigs on top. It will be a beautifully creamy almond colour.

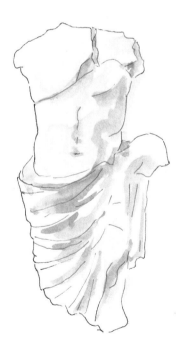

MIRABILE VISU
Wonderful to behold

CHAPTER TWO
Green Salads and Vegetables

APICIAN LENTILS AND CHESTNUTS

The Ingredients

Five tablespoons of green Puy lentils

Three ounces of cooked chestnuts

A handful of spinach

Generous rounds of sea salt and pepper

A tablespoon of coriander seed

A teaspoon of honey

A little butter and olive oil

A tablespoon of zesty balsamic vinegar

I teaspoon of paprika

I chicken stock cube dissolved in a pint of water

I medium sized onion, finely sliced

Some fresh sprigs of mint for decoration

Preparation Time: 5 minutes
Cooking Time: 45 minutes
Serves: 4 – 6 guests as an accompanying dish

Lenticchie e Castagne de Apicius

*

LENTICULAM ET CASTINEIS APICIUS

This is a very wholesome and nutritional repast. Lentils are high in vitamins and low in calories. The chestnuts provide an earthy, nutty partner. The combination of pulses and chestnuts were popular in classical times and are still today with Italian epicureans particularly in Campania. The ingredients are inexpensive and readily available.

Simmer the lentils for 30 minutes in plentiful salted water. Then lift off the frothy surface if you have one with a spoon. Sweat the onions over a very low heat in a little butter and oil for 3 minutes until they reach a translucent colour.

Then add the cooked chestnuts, paprika, coriander seed, honey and stock together with a drizzle of the balsamic vinegar. Grind in the salt and pepper.

Simmer for a further 5 minutes, no longer so that the chestnuts retain their innate crunchiness. The cooking liqueur should reduce to a pleasant but not too mushy pulp. Drain the residue liquid if necessary.

Shred the spinach and mix in with the dish and then scatter with mint on top and serve to your appreciative guests.

CENABIS BENE
You will dine well

33

CELERIAC AND PARSNIP PUREE

The Ingredients

One small celeriac

Two parsnips

The zest of one lemon

One chicken stock cube

Two ounces of butter

Ten grinds of black pepper

A little salt

Parsley

Virgin olive oil

Preparation Time: 10 Minutes
Cooking Time: 40 minutes
Serves: 4

Sedano Rapa e Pastinaca

*

CELERIAC IUS ET PASTINACA

Peel the celeriac and parsnips and poach in hot water with the zest of lemon and some of the salt and pepper for 40 minutes.

Then smash and mash with the butter and add the parsley.

Drizzle with olive oil.

And serve.

POSSUNT QUIA POSSE VIDIENTUR
They can do it because they can

GOAT'S CHEESE OMELETTE SOUFFLÉ WITH SORREL AND PARSLEY

The Ingredients

Six eggs

Two egg whites (separate from the six eggs)

One round of goat's cheese

Six ounces of sorrel, finely chopped

A medium handful of parsley, finely chopped

Two tablespoons of greek yogurt

Butter and oil

Salt and pepper and parsley to decorate

Prep. Time: 5 minutes
Cooking Time: 8 minutes
Serves: 4 for a starter
And 2 for a light supper

Omelette Soufflé Con Formaggio di Capra Sorrel e Prezzemelo

*

OVA SPHONGIA CUM CASEUM CAPRAE, LAPATHUM ET APIUM

Whisk together the six eggs and season with salt and pepper. Separate the remaining two eggs and whisk the whites until they are stiff. If you do have a copper pan in which to do this the metal helps to ensure they are fluffier and lighter to suck in the air. Meanwhile prepare herbs and slice up the goat's cheese including the rind and sauté in some butter on a very gentle heat for a few minutes.

Fold the egg whites into the egg yolk mixture and heat up the butter and oil to a moderate heat.

Whilst this is foaming, give the pan a good shake and then tip in the soufflé and cook for a few minutes. Then add the goat's cheese, herbs and yogurt and cook for a further minute or two.

The mixture in the middle should remain runny so watch the pan carefully.

Then tip the omelette on to a large platter and deck with parsley

Cut into slices and serve.

Eggs were often served at the beginning of meal as an appetiser in classical times. Not unsurprisingly, eggs were believed to be an aid to fertility. As Pliny writes:

When Julia Augustus was pregnant with Tiberius Caesar, by Nero, she wanted a boy and so she followed the divination believed by young women. She kept an egg close to her chest and when she has to set it aside, she gave to the nurse to keep it warm. It worked!

AD PRAESENS OVA CRAS PULLIS SUNT MELIORA
Eggs today are better than chickens tomorrow

Or our present saying: A bird in the hand is worth two in the bush

Meaning: advice for risk takers, hold onto what you have rather than risk everything.

PASTA IN A WALNUT PARMESAN SAUCE

The Ingredients

Five ounces of pasta – penne, spaghetti or pasta bows – all will do nicely

Two ounces of cream cheese

Two tablespoons of grated Parmesan

Two ounces of crushed walnuts

A quarter of a pint of single cream

Olive oil

A little lemon juice

Sea salt and pepper

Torn oregano and chives to garnish

Boil up a large pan of water adding a little salt. Cook the pasta until *al dente* – about 10 minutes.

In the meantime – make up the sauce.

Heat the cream cheese gently and stir in the cream. Then add the grated Parmesan, salt and pepper.

It will take just a few minutes.

Drain your pasta and add the olive oil and lemon juice, give it a good toss and melt in the cream cheese and Parmesan sauce.

Sprinkle with the crushed walnuts, oregano and chives.

Particularly good with some icy chilled white wine.

PROSIT
Cheers

This is a Latin toast meaning 'To your good fortune and to life'.

SPIRITED SWEET PEA PUDDINGS

The Ingredients

Eight ounces of peas, shelled if fresh or frozen

Two ounces of butter

One shallot finely chopped

Two eggs separated

One ounce of plain flour

One quarter of a pint of milk

A few slivers of ham

Salt and pepper

A teaspoon of icing sugar

Preparation Time: 15 minutes
Cooking Time: 25 minutes
Serves: 4 for a starter or a light supper

Sollerate Budini Pisello Dolce

*

FABA DULCE CUM ANIMA

Cook the peas in some salted water for three minutes and drain.

Put the butter and the shallot in a pan and simmer for another few minutes. Add the flour and ham and stir well until quite thickened. Then mix in the peas, salt and pepper and icing sugar.

Pour in the milk and a give your mixture a good swish with a whisk.

Cool slightly and beat in the egg yolks.

Preheat your oven to 200 degrees.

Stiff up the egg whites in a blender or with a fork. They need to be high and fluffy.

Divide your mixture between four lightly buttered soufflé dishes folding in the egg whites last.

And then bake in your preheated oven for about 25 minutes until risen and golden.

Serve immediately.

AB OVO USQUE AD MALA
From the beginning of the egg
and
From start to finish

TUSCAN TRUFFLES WITH WILD MUSHROOMS

The Ingredients

Six ounces of mushrooms, chanterelles, boletuses, chestnut

Four teaspoons of black or white truffles

One clove of garlic

Three ounces of red wine

One ounce of olive oil

A generous handful of parsley

A sprinkling of salt and pepper

Preparation Time: One hour to marinate
Cooking Time: 15 minutes
Serves: 4 for a starter

Tartufi Toscani con Funghi Dibosco

*

BOLETUS FUNGAS CUM TUBERA

Marinate the mushrooms in 1 ounce of the red wine to allow the mushrooms to lap up the wine. Really any combination of mushrooms you can lay your hands on will work but my suggestion as above I would recommend. The dish and looks and tastes rather exotic.

Then add most of the parsley and garlic.

Retain some parsley for an illustrious finish.

Then add the truffles or truffle sauce, salt and pepper and sauté in the olive oil and remaining red wine for 5 – 6 minutes.

Decorate with the remaining parsley.

Truffle sauce is a little cheaper than a jar of truffles and still gives you an exotic flavour with the combination of the earthy mushrooms.

Mushrooms and truffles were also known be a reliable aphrodisiac so may the gods be with you, especially Venus.

ROMANI QUIDEM ARTEM AMATORIAM INVENERENT
The Romans invented the art of love.

APUDNE TE VEL ME
Your place or mine?

DEEP FRIED ARTICHOKE HEARTS

The Ingredients

One jar or tin of artichoke hearts

One and a half ounces of plain flour

One egg separated

One tablespoon of olive oil

A few ounces of water

Black pepper and sea salt

Sunflower oil for the deep frying

Watercress for a flourishing finish

Preparation Time: 10 minutes
Cooking Time: 5 minutes
Serves: 4

Carciofi Fritti

*

CARDUOS FRICTA

Drain the artichoke hearts and cut up in small halves.

Put the flour into a bowl with a little salt and then add the separated egg yolk and oil.

Beat for a few minutes adding the water. Then whisk up the egg white until it forms snowy peaks.

Fold into the batter using a metal spoon.

Heat up the sunflower oil at about 180° and when bubbling dip the artichokes into the batter, coat thoroughly and fry for two minutes.

No longer so that they emerge with a golden glow.

Serve immediately on a bed of watercress.

PENETRALIA MENTIS
Heart of hearts

SALAD OF AVOCADO, CUCUMBER AND KIWI

The Ingredients

Two ripe avocados

The juice of one lemon

One cucumber

One kiwi fruit

Four tablespoons of olive oil

One teaspoon of caster sugar

One teaspoon of honey

Sea salt and pepper and chopped fresh mint

Preparation Time: 15 minutes
Serves: 4 for a starter

Avocado Cetrioli e Ensalata di Kiwi

＊

KIWI FRUCTUM CUCUMIS AVOCADO ET ACETARIA

Swish up and blend the olive oil, caster sugar and honey adding the sea salt and pepper.

Peel and stone the avocados and immerse in the lemon juice to prevent discolouration.

Then trim the cucumber and kiwi fruit and slice up thinly.

Arrange the avocado, cucumber and kiwi into a fan shape and toss over the dressing of the olive oil, sugar and honey.

Decorate with the mint and serve.

USUS PROMPTOS FACIT
Practice makes perfect

RISOTTO RING WITH PRAWNS AND SAMPHIRE

The Ingredients

Six ounces of Italian risotto rice

Four ounces of Atlantic prawns

A handful of samphire or if not in season the same of spinach

One ounce of butter

Half a pint of chicken stock

Half a pint of white wine

One small onion, shredded

One garlic clove

Parmesan cheese

Sea salt and pepper

Sprigs of dill and snipped chives

Preparation Time: 10 minutes
Cooking Time: 30 minutes
Serves: 4

Anello Risotto con Gamberi e Samphire

*

ORBIS RISOTTO CUM PISCE ET BATIS GENERATIM

Melt the butter in a pan with the shredded onion and garlic clove for a few minutes until softened.

Add the chicken stock and white wine and of course the rice.

Season with sea salt and pepper.

Simmer for 25 minutes until the rice is tender and the liquid absorbed.

Mix in the samphire or torn spinach and the prawns for about 3 minutes.

When done serve with the grated Parmesan cheese and garnish with the dill and chives.

FAMA VOLAT
Rumour travels fast

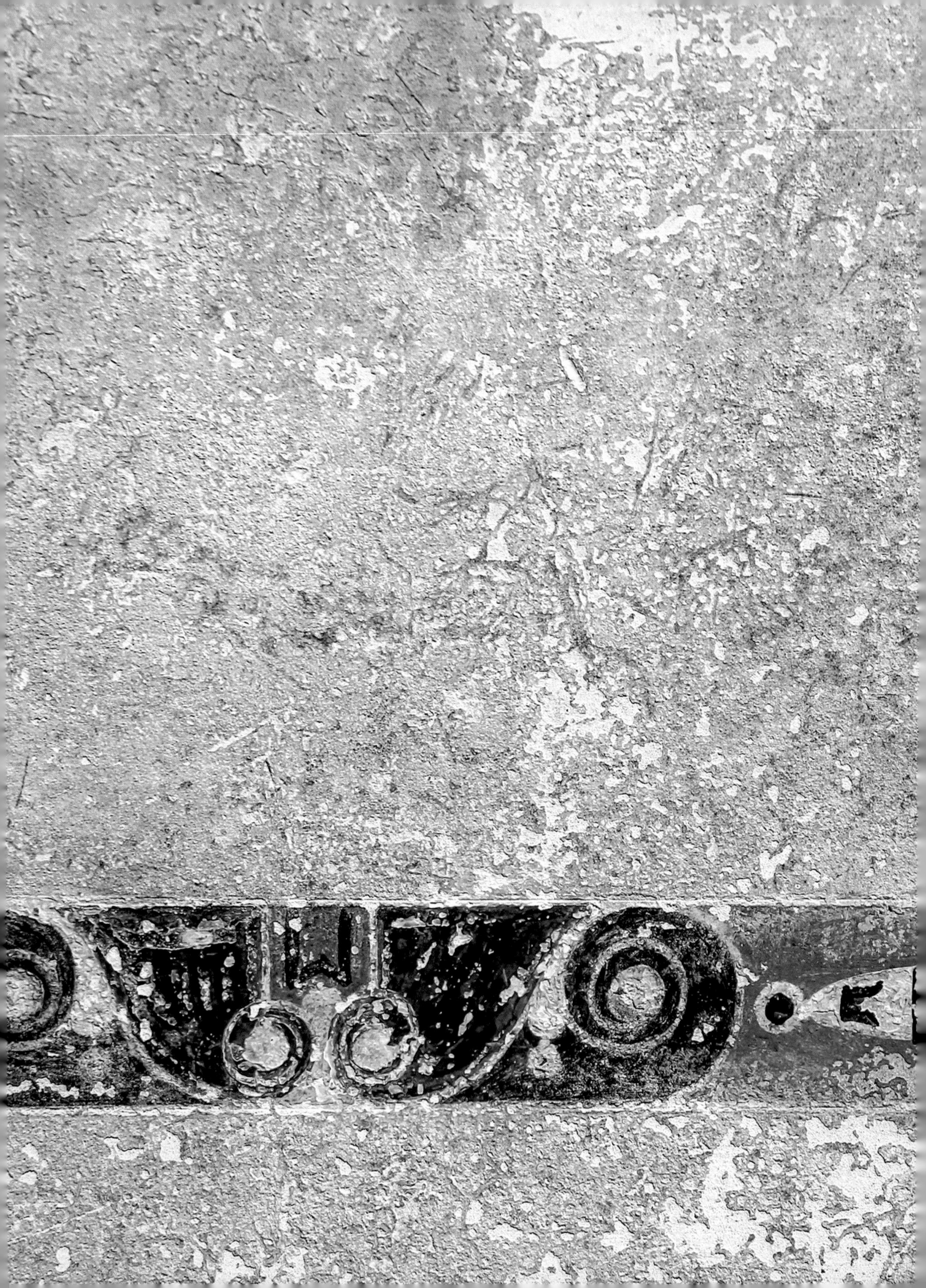

CHAPTER THREE

Main Course
Meat and Game

LEGOVER LAMB WITH ANCHOVIES AND LAVENDER

The Ingredients

A leg of lamb

Four ounces of fresh anchovies

A small handful of crushed lavender flowers

Olive oil and garlic

Six crushed juniper berries

A little flour, sea salt and pepper

A quarter of a pint of red wine and the same of rosé wine

Preparation Time: 2 hours
Cooking Time: One and a half hours
Resting Time: 20 minutes
Serves: 4 – 6

Agnello rimasto con Acciughe e Lavanda

*

RELIQUUMAGNUS CUM APUA ET LAVANDA

Marinate the lamb in half of the red and rosé wine and the crushed juniper berries for a few hours, the longer the better.

Remove the lamb and dust down with a little flour. Then sear in some hot olive oil for 10 minutes until browned. Leave to cool and then stab with some garlic and tuck in the anchovies and the lavender – just the flowers not the stalks. If you cannot lamentably lay your hands on fresh anchovies – don't despair – use tinned anchovy fillets instead. You will still impress your guests.

Heat the oven to 170° and place the lamb in your oven pan and immerse it in the rest of the red and rosé wine. Grind over your sea salt and pepper and put in the oven for an hour and a half.

Then you will have produced a darkly handsome lamb leg with pink meat in the middle for your guests who prefer it like that. The addition of rosé wine gives the lamb a sweeter flavour and the red wine gives it a ruby be-jewelled colour.

You would think that the anchovies would overpower the lamb but they don't – they disappear into an unctuous elixir. The lavender gives the lamb a fragrant flavour.

When your princely lamb is cooked – leave it to rest for 20 minutes.

Then carve up and serve with the wine gravy and some green vegetables.

Lentils and chestnuts also accompany very well.

IBI NON ERIT RELIQUIAS
There won't be any leftovers

CRISPY DUCK WITH HONEY AND ALMONDS ON A BLANKET OF TURNIPS WITH A HARICOT BEAN AND CRANBERRY DRESSING

The Ingredients

Four duck legs or duck breasts or a mixture of both

One pound of turnips

Goose fat

Two tablespoons of honey

Two tablespoons of crushed almonds

Sea salt

The haricot bean and cranberry dressing

Three ounces of haricot beans

One tablespoon of cranberry

A quarter pint of chicken stock

A big splash of balsamic vinegar

Asparagus spears

Thyme

Preparation Time: 10 Minutes
Cooking Time: One Hour
Serves: 4

Anatra Croccante su una Coperta di Rape

*

CRISPUS ANATEM EX RAPIS

Dust the duck with sea salt and leave for a few hours.

Then wash the salt off and let the duck dry for half an hour. This will tenderise the duck and help it on its way to be nice and crispy.

Then prick the duck and anoint with the honey and crushed almonds. Heat up the oven to 180° and add the goose fat.

Whilst the oven is coming up to temperature, prepare and peel the turnips and put them in the chicken stock. Simmer for half an hour. Then slice them up.

Put the duck in the oven for about 50 minutes. When the turnips are cooked, add to the duck so they can all roast together for the last 20 minutes.

Whilst cooking, prepare the haricot bean dressing. Simmer the beans in the chicken stock and balsamic vinegar with the thyme for 15 minutes.

Take out the duck to rest and blanch the asparagus spears for a few minutes.

Plate up the honeyed almond duck on the blanket of turnips. If you are serving duck breast, slice to reveal the pink tender meat and if you have duck legs, leave as they are. Then serve with the haricot dressing with the asparagus spears on top.

EIUSDEM FAINAE
Birds of a feather

ROSEMARY PHEASANT IN A JUNIPER AND TRUFFLE SAUCY SAUCE

The Ingredients

Two pheasants

Two tablespoons of crushed rosemary

The zest of one lemon and one lime

A tablespoon of goose fat

Two ounces of butter

Sea salt and black pepper

Parsley for decoration

The saucy sauce

Ten crushed juniper berries

Two black truffles

Half a pint of white wine and the same of beef stock

Preparation Time: 5 minutes
Cooking Time: One Hour and 15 Minutes
Serves: 4

Fagiano di Rosemarino Salsa Impertinente di Ginepro et Tartufo

*

ROSE CONDIMENTUM PHARSIANO IUNIPERI ET TUBER PETULANTIAM

Heat the oven to 180° and give the pheasants a massage with the goose fat and butter. Then rub in the zest of the lime and lemon. Sprinkle with the rosemary, sea salt and pepper.

Sear the pheasants for a few minutes until lightly bronzed then immerse in a casserole pot for an hour and 15minutes.

Meanwhile, make up the juniper and truffle sauce

Easy-peasy – crush the juniper berries, add the truffles and the wine and stock and simmer for half an hour. Taste and add salt and pepper if you need additional flavouring.

Take the pheasants out after cooking and leave to breathe for 5 minutes and then carve up, plate up with the sauce and decorate with the fronds of parsley.

Pheasant exudes a sweet and earthy flavour and the juniper and truffle saucy sauce is a happy partner.

This dish is best served with cavola nero and hazelnuts.

AD GUSTUM
To one's taste

CHICKEN BREASTS WITH PORCINI AND PANCETTA IN A WATERCRESS SAUCE

The Ingredients

Four chicken breasts

Two oz of porcini

Four slices of pancetta

The zest of one lemon

Olive oil

Sea salt and black pepper

The watercress sauce

One bunch of watercress and a small handful of mint

A quarter of a pint of chicken stock

Two tablespoons of double cream

One tablespoon of butter

Two cloves of garlic, crushed

Preparation Time: 10 minutes
Cooking Time: One Hour
Serves: 4 welcome guests

Petti di Pollo con Funghi Porcini e Pancetta in una Salsa di Crestione

*

UBERA PORCINI ET PULLUM CUM LARDUM CONDIMENTUM IN SISYMBRIUM

Firstly, mix the olive oil and lemon zest over the chicken breasts and shower with a little sea salt and pepper.

Wrap with the pancetta and tuck in the porcini.

Immerse into the oven at 180° and then cook the watercress sauce.

Simmer the watercress in the chicken stock and after 10 minutes add the double cream, butter and garlic. Then keep warm to serve with the chicken.

Decorate with the mint.

Best served with a crisp, light wine.

CARPE DIEM
Seize the day

(Taken from Horace's Odes.)

CHICKEN WITH LEMON SQUASH AND MARK'S WALNUT AND HONEY VINAIGRETTE

The Ingredients

One plump medium sized chicken

One butternut squash peeled and sliced up

One shallot

Two lemons one for the drizzle and one for mark's walnut and honey melt

Olive oil

A handful of coriander and parsley

Butter and olive oil

Mark's walnut and honey melt

A tablespoon of balsamic vinegar

A teaspoon of grainy mustard

Three tablespoons of walnut oil

The zest and juice of one lemon

Preparation Time: 20 minutes
Cooking Time: An hour and a half
10 minutes to wait for the Chicken to rest
Serves: 4

First sweat the squash and the shallot with the lemon zest of one of the lemons and a little butter for 15 minutes on a low heat. Meanwhile give the chicken a body rub with the rest of the butter and the olive oil and throw some salt and pepper at it. Then stuff the chicken with the squash, coriander and parsley and squeeze the lemon juice from the other lemon over it.

Put in the oven for an hour and a half. Baste and let rest for 15 minutes.

Whilst this is cooking, whisk up the walnut oil, honey, balsamic vinegar and mustard with the rest of the lemon juice for the vinaigrette and then when ready to serve warm it up.

Carve the chicken and serve with green vegetables and the walnut and honey lemon vinaigrette.

FAMES OPTIMUM CONDIMENTUM
Hunger is the best seasoning

BLUEBERRY VENISON

The Ingredients

One and a half pounds of diced venison

A punnet of blueberries

Ten crushed juniper berries

One tablespoon of fennel seed

A quarter pint of red wine

And a quarter pint of beef stock

One tablespoon of cornflour

Sea salt and black pepper and fresh mint

Preparation Time: 5 minutes
Cooking Time: One Hour and 15 minutes
Serves: 4

Herpothamnus Cervinae

*

HERPOTHAMNUS CERVAE

Dust the venison in the cornflour and fennel seed.

Add the crushed juniper berries and sea salt and pepper.

Then heat up the red wine and beef stock and immerse the venison and half of the blueberries in a casserole dish straight to the oven at 180°.

After 40 minutes of the cooking time add the rest of the blueberries.

When finished and seasoned according to your taste, garnish with the fresh mint and serve.

It is good with celeriac and parsnip puree.

QUALIS PATER, TALIS FILIUS
Like father, like son

(Like my boys, Mark and Marcus.)

STAGGERING VENISON WRAPPED IN PROSCIUTTO WITH QUINCE AND JUNIPER

The Ingredients

Two to three pounds of haunch of venison

Six fine slices of prosciutto

20 Crushed juniper berries

A pint of red wine

Olive oil

Oregano leaves

A generous sprinkling of balsamic vinegar

Four quinces or quince jelly

A spoonful of runny honey

Sea salt flakes and grindings of pepper

Parsley and / or mint for decoration

Preparation:20 minutes for the venison and the quince sauce
Marinate for: 2-3 hours
Cooking Time: one and a half hours at 180°
Serves: 4

First of all, I apologise for the title, but I cannot help myself.

Making little incisions, spike the venison with the crushed juniper berries. Sprinkle with sea salt and pepper and drizzle over the olive oil.

Then immerse in a bath of red wine, oregano leaves and olive oil, sea salt flakes and pepper. Marinate for 2 – 3 hours.

When ready to cook, remove the marinade and keep aside for the wine gravy. Heat up the oven to 200° to begin with and sear the venison in a deep casserole pot for 10 minutes and then turn down the heat to 180°for approximately one hour, checking the joint so as not to over-cook and keeping some pink meat in the middle of the saddle.

Halfway through cooking, take the joint out to rest for a few minutes and then wrap around the prosciutto. Put back in the oven and meanwhile prepare the quince sauce.

Peel and cut up the quinces and simmer for 15 minutes with the runny honey and balsamic vinegar. If you cannot find quinces, cheat and just buy quince jelly.

Take out the venison when done and warm up the wine gravy.

Good to leave the venison to rest for 10 minutes.

Carve up the venerable venison and throw some herbs, the parsley and mint around it for flavour and decoration and serve with the quince sauce.

CORNU COPIAE
Horn of plenty

BRISKET OF BEEF WITH JUNIPER BERRIES, BLACK ONION SEEDS, STEEPED IN A RED WINE ELIXIR

The Ingredients

Rib of beef brisket – two to three pounds

Olive oil rub

Corn flour

A few cloves of garlic

Ten juniper berries, crushed

Some thyme (we all need it)

A goodly handful of black onion seeds and parsley to decorate

Coarse sea salt and ten grindings of pepper

Half a pint of red wine and an additional half pint of beef stock

Preparation Time: 10 minutes
Cooking Time: 2 Hours
Serves: 4 guests

Petto di Manzo con ginepro e semi dicipolla nero ricco Un elixir divino Rosa

*

BUBULAE CUM CEPA SEMINA JUNIPERA ET INEBRIARE VIN IUS

Preheat the oven to 180° for 15 minutes.

Spike the beef with the garlic cloves. And then give the beef a body rub of olive oil and the corn flour. Grind over the pepper and salt.

Mix up the wine, stock, thyme, crushed juniper berries and onion seeds.

Immerse your beef in this elixir and put in the oven. If you have a clay-pot – that is perfect, I find. Or if not, a deep casserole dish.

Cook for 2 hours and then take it out and let it breathe for 10 minutes.

Carve up, decorate with parsley and enjoy.

This crown of beef is best served with a good red wine.

ARBITER BIBENDI
A toastmaster

VEAL ESCALOPES WITH MARSALA AND CREAMY WILD MUSHROOMS

The Ingredients

Four escalopes of veal

Wild mushrooms

Three tablespoons of marsala

Four tablespoons of double cream

One tablespoon of seasoned flour

Parmesan cheese grated

Olive oil and butter

Fresh marjoram

Preparation Time: 15 minutes
Cooking Time: 20 minutes
Serves: 4

Scaloppine di Vitello al Marsala e Selvatica Funghi

*

VITULI ET FERA FUNGOS CUM MARSALA

Coat the veal escalopes in the seasoned flour. Warm up the butter and oil and then add the mushrooms and cook for a few minutes and then set aside.

Heat up a little more oil and butter to a moderate heat and sink in the veal with some of the marjoram. Stir in the marsala and the cream.

Cook for 15 minutes, tossing and turning to baste evenly. Halfway through cooking add the mushrooms. Grate the Parmesan cheese over the veal and lightly grill for a few minutes.

Then serve with a garnish of marjoram.

Best with a few glasses of light white wine to wash this fabulous supper down.

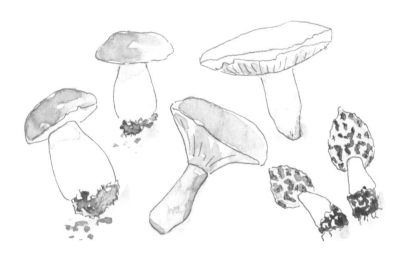

NE QUID NIMIS
Nothing in excess

HAM IN GINGERBREAD WITH A BARLEY WINE

The Ingredients

The Ham

Two and a half lb of gammon ham

Ten figs (keep five back for final decoration)

Black onion seeds

Five rounds each of salt and pepper

Asparagus

The gingerbread

Four ounces of plain flour

A pinch of salt

Two ounces of butter

Two ounces of grated ginger

One beaten egg

A little water

The Barley Wine

Ten ounces of red wine

Two tablespoons of barley

One beef stock cube

A few sprigs of rosemary

To decorate

Fresh figs and leafy herbs

Asparagus

Preparation Time: An hour and a half to simmer the ham, 10 minutes to let it rest
10 minutes to prepare the Gingerbread then refrigerate whilst the ham is cooking
5 minutes to whizz together the Barley Wine
Cooking Time: 30 minutes for the Ham in Gingerbread to bake
Serves: 4

Prosciutto in Pan di Zenzero Conil Vino D'Orzo

*

MUSTEIS PETASONEM

Firstly, remove the rind from the ham and secure with string. Boil up a pan of water and add the figs and black onion seeds. When the boiling water is at its zenith, then immerse the ham and turn down the heat to simmer for an hour and a half or so.

Meanwhile you can prepare the gingerbread.

Sift the flour well and rub in the butter using your fingertips which helps ensure the pastry is light and fluffy. Add the grated ginger and give it all a good massage. Put your pastry in the fridge until the ham is ready which makes it easier to roll out.

You can now prepare the barley wine. Put the red wine in a pan with the barley and cook on a medium heat for 20 minutes. Add the stock cube and rosemary after 10 minutes. Give it a good stir.

The outcome should be a generous jus, not too thin and not too thick. Adjust as you think fit.

When the ham is cooked then let it rest for 10 minutes whilst you roll out your gingerbread pastry.

Envelop the ham with the gingerbread and paint it with the beaten egg, then put in the oven at 180° for half an hour.

When your porcine beauty is ready, leave him for a few minutes before you carve and in between blanch the asparagus.

Carve and serve with the exuberant barley wine.

This is a marvellously rich and exotic dish with the molten ginger exploding through the pastry. And perfectly complimented with al dente asparagus.

NULLA MENSA SINE IMPENSA
There's no such thing as a free lunch

CHAPTER FOUR
PISCEAN FISH DISHES

PINKER THAN PINK PRAWNS IN A GRENADINE SAUCE

The Ingredients

Four ounces of Atlantic prawns

Four tablespoons of mayonnaise

Two tablespoons of Italian tomato puree

Two generous tablespoons of grenadine

One tablespoon of lemon juice

A little sea salt and pepper

Crisp lettuce and rocket leaves

A few strands of dill

Serves: 4 for a starter

Rosa Gamberoni Rosa su Salsa Granatina

*

ROSEA QUAM ROSA SQUILLAE CUM GRENADINE CONDIMENTUM

To start…

Mix the mayonnaise and tomato puree together with the prawns

And then add the grenadine and lemon juice.

Another good stir

Grind in the sea salt and pepper.

If you cannot lay your hands on grenadine in your store cupboard or wine cellar, pomegranate or cranberry juices are happy and able substitutes.

I serve this salad in cocktail glasses, they look celebratory and stylish.

Tear the lettuce and rocket leaves and place in your glasses. Spoon the prawn, mayonnaise, tomato puree, grenadine and lemon juice atop and place straight in the fridge.

When ready to serve, garnish with the dill.

AD INGUEM ROSA
Perfectly Pink

This phrase translates as "to a fingernail", meaning to accomplish well and with precision. Sculptors in Classical times would run a fingernail over their masterpieces to test for smoothness.

SCALLOPS IN A PROSECCO AND SAFFRON SAUCE

The Ingredients

Twelve scallops

A quarter of a pint of Prosecco

A few strands of saffron

Zest of a lime and the juice

Two tablespoons of yogurt

Two tablespoons of double cream

Walnut oil

Sea salt and black pepper

A little fresh oregano

A green salad

Olive oil and apple balsamic dressing

Preparation Time: 15 minutes
Cooking Time: 10 minutes
Serves: 4

Capesante in una Salsa di Prosecco e Zefferani

*

PECTINES IN PROSECCO ET CROCUS CONDIMENTUM

Discard the scallops' coral – if you have it and marinate the scallops in the lime zest and juice for 10 minutes. The lime will tenderise the scallops without swamping the delicate flavour of the scallops.

Any fish dish should be revered and not eclipsed by a heavy halo of ingredients.

Next, prepare the sauce mixing the yogurt and cream with the saffron and Prosecco.

Simmer over a low heat for 5 minutes so that the saffron can breathe and allow the sauce to exude a golden colour. Then keep it warm.

Whizz up the apple balsamic vinegar with the olive oil. If you cannot find apple balsamic in a delicatessen – add apple juice to the vinegar – it works just as well.

Heat up a griddle pan to a moderate temperature in the walnut oil. Add the scallops when the heat is up so that they can sizzle away for 5 minutes grinding in the sea salt and pepper. Scallops should never be over-cooked so if you have an enthusiastic top oven – grill for a couple of minutes less.

When they are ready – plate up and anoint with the Prosecco and saffron sauce and decorate with the oregano.

Serve with a green salad and the apple balsamic dressing which will give the dish a kick and balance the creamy sauce.

FINE PISCIUM FACIT BONUM PATINA
A fine fish makes a good dish

LUSTY LOBSTER CAKES

The Ingredients

Two fine lobsters cooked – better than going through the trauma of boiling

One beaten egg

A medium pinch of saffron

A small handful of breadcrumbs

A little butter and olive oil

Parsley

Sea salt and pepper

Preparation Time: 10 minutes
Cooking Time: 20 minutes
Serves: 4

So to the sea:

Eke out the lobster meat from every crevice.

Set aside the shells for a future bisque – a sin to waste them and you can always freeze.

Warm up the butter and oil and the bread crumbs, saffron and egg yolk and add your lobster meat, sea salt and pepper.

Not too frenetically with your stirring so as not to separate the lobster.

Shape into cakes and dust with flour.

Cover with a plate and put in the fridge to firm up.

Dust with a little more flour before frying.

Cook in a pan with a moderation of the rest of the oil and butter for 10 minutes, turning so you can enjoy the pale golden colour and faintly crispiness.

FELICITAS HABET MULTOS AMICOS
Properity has Many Friends

When life is going swimmingly, we do not lack friends,

When our fortunes turn – you know who your true friends are.

MARK'S SHELL BAY OYSTERS WITH BALSAMIC VINEGAR, OLIVE OIL, GARLIC AND CHILLI

The Ingredients

Eight oysters and one for luck in case one doesn't want to open, in which case you discard

Two tablespoons of balsamic vinegar

A little sprinkling of olive oil

One clove of crushed garlic

Two teaspoons of Tabasco

Preparation Time: 10 minutes
Cooking Time: None
Serves: For a pre- Dinner Aperitif

Marco Bay Testa Ostreae cum Aceto, Allium et Oleum Oliva e Tabasco

*

MARCO OSTRICHE CUM ACETO BALSAMINUS, ALLIUM ET OLEUM OLIVA TABASCO

First you have to shuck the oysters. The best way to do this is to put the oysters on a wooden board.

Stab with a sharp knife at the hinge which is the narrowest point of the shell.

When the hinge breaks you can then lift out the oyster meat.

Mix up the balsamic vinegar, olive oil, crushed garlic and the Tabasco.

Give it a good shake.

Then spoon the oyster back into the shells and add your balsamic vinaigrette.

Chill for 5 minutes and serve with a chilled glass of white wine.

NON TENEAS TOTUM QUOD SPLENDIT UT AURUM
All that glitters is not gold

PINK SEA BREAM IN AN APPLE AND HORSERADISH CREAM

The Ingredients

For the fish

Four fillets of pink sea bream

The zest and juice of a lemon

Two ounces of melted butter

Sea salt and pepper

Sprigs of dill and or chives

The apple and horseradish cream

One apple cored and skinned

Two tablespoons of horseradish – freshly grated or sauce

Three tablespoons of double cream

Preparation Time: Marinate the sea bream in the lemon zest for half an hour
Cooking Time: For the fish and the apple and horseradish cream –
20 minutes cooked simultaneously
Serves: 4

Crema Rosa Orata una Mela e Refano

*

ROSA PISCES CUM POMUM IUS

First step: make sure the sea bream has been filleted but keep the skin on as it gives the fish a cosy blanket when cooking and a crispy finish.

Shower with the juice of the lemon and the zest and dust with

Sea salt and pepper.

Add the melted butter.

Wrap in foil and warm up the oven to 150°. Immerse the fish into the oven when you have prepared the apple cream as both dishes take the same *length of time.*

The Apple and Horseradish Cream

Slice up the apple finely and simmer in a small amount of water for 20 minutes also. When melted add the horseradish and the double cream and keep warm.

After the combined 20 minutes of cooking time, lift the sea bream out and divest it of its foil.

Plate up with the apple and horseradish cream and crown with some dill and chives.

QUI ME AMAT ET PISCES MEAM
Love me, love my piscean dishes

HALIBUT IN VANILLA BUTTER

The Ingredients

Four fillets of halibut

One apple scored, peeled and finely sliced

One vanilla stick

Three ounces of butter

Two generous tablespoons of double cream

Half a juice of lemon

Salt and pepper

Dill and capers

Preparation Time: 10 minutes
Cooking Time: 15 minutes
Serves: 4

Halibut in un Elisir di Mela e Vaniglia

*

HIPPOGLOSSUS PER MALUM IUS ET VANILLA

Marinate the halibut fillets for 5 minutes in the lemon juice, salt and pepper.

Warm up the double cream with the vanilla stick for 5 minutes. Leave to cool.

Meanwhile cook half of the butter gently with the sliced apple for 10 minutes until nice and smooth.

Heat a pan with the remaining butter and when up to temperature as you think fit. Fry the halibut fillets for about 7 minutes, dousing with a little more salt and pepper.

Mix the apple with the cream and vanilla and warm up.

Serve the halibut with the apple and vanilla cream sauce and adorn with dill and capers.

AUREO HAMO PISCARI
Money Talks

This adage means that any door can be opened by gold.

SALMON FILLET WITH GINGER AND DILL IN A SORREL VELOUTÉ

The Ingredients

Four Salmon fillets

One shallot, spliced

A large handful of sorrel

(Spinach if you cannot lay your hands on sorrel)

Two Ounces of butter

Some dill

Chopped ginger

One tablespoon of icing sugar

Four tablespoons of double cream

Sea salt and pepper

Preparation Time: 30 minutes then the salmon can marinate quietly for an hour
Cooking Time: 20 minutes
Serves: 4

Filetto di Salmone con Zenzero e Aneto e una Vellutata Sorrel

*

PISCE FASCIA INFULA GINGERBERI ET ANETHUM CUM IUS LAPATHUM

Douse the salmon fillet in the dill and ginger and marinate for an hour.

Turn on the oven to 180° and when up to temperature, place the salmon in foil in the oven with the ounce of butter and cook for 15 – 20 minutes.

Meanwhile, make up the sorrel sauce. Sorrel is not always easy to find but you can buy a plant in your local nursery or order on-line, it grows like the clappers and looks lovely in your herb garden or your window box.

Sorrel does have an exquisite and very different taste so it is worth the effort. If this is not possible – replace with spinach in the same cooking manner.

Warm up the other ounce of the butter, add the shallot and cook gently for a few minutes so that it retains its pale translucent colour. Shred the sorrel or spinach, season with the sea salt and pepper and add the double cream and icing sugar. The icing sugar turns the sauce into a frothy velouté icing.

Then whisk up for a few minutes until you have a mossy green sauce.

Take out the salmon which should be pink and not over-cooked and pour over the joyous sorrel velouté.

MAGIS MUTUS QUAM PISCIS
Quieter than a fish

CHAPTER FIVE
LA DOLCE VITA

POMPEIAN PEARS POACHED IN PROSECCO

The Ingredients

Four Nice pears

Half a bottle of Prosecco

One ounce of sugar and a thinly pared rind of one lemon

Preparation Time: Two Minutes
Cooking Time: Ten Minutes
Serves: 4

Pere Pompeiani in Camicia a Prosecco

*

PIRA CUM PROSECCO

Take four nice pears and immerse them in a pan of boiling water for one minute. Then cool them immediately in iced water to prevent more cooking. Warm up your Prosecco, sugar and lemon rind. Immerse your pears upstanding in this mix and simmer for a few minutes.

You can chill in the fridge until your guests arrive and serve with your usual undoubted grace.

FRUCTUS AMORIS
Fruit of love

EVA'S TUSCAN PRALINE CAKE

The Ingredients

Four ounces of butter

One tablespoon of golden syrup

Two dessert spoons of cocoa

A large dark chocolate bar – about 4 ounces

Half a pound of amaretto biscuits

Toscana Praline torta di Eva

*

EVA IN TUSCI PRALINE

This dessert never fails to deliver to chocolate lovers, (mostly girls).

I have re-created Aunty Eva's magical pudding for many children's teas and dinner parties and it never fails to vanish within minutes.

It is also incredibly simple to prepare and literally, a piece of heavenly cake.

Heat the butter, the golden syrup and cocoa over a low heat. Melt the chocolate over a bowl of water until completely liquid. Pound the amaretto biscuits and stir in well with the butter, syrup and cocoa. Prepare a tin with lightly buttered baking paper. Place the divine mixture into the tin and pour over the chocolate elixir.

Set in the fridge for an hour. Wait until it is cold and set.

Then cut up into pieces and it is then ready to go to the table (but not for long…)

BONUM ENIM EST ANIMA SCELERISQUE
Chocolate is good for the soul

ALMOND CREAM CASANOVA WITH STRAWBERRIES AND MARASCHINO

The Ingredients

Three ounces of mascarpone cheese

Two ounces of crushed almonds

One ounce of icing sugar

Sliced strawberries

Maraschino

Preparation Time: 15 minutes
Serves: 4

Crema di Mandorli Casanova con Fragoli e Marashischino

*

CREMOR CUM FRAGA ET AMYGDALINAS MARASCHINO

This is a very simple but effective and delightful dessert.

Cooking doesn't always need to be complicated.

Whip up the mascarpone with a whisk and add the crushed almonds.

Add the icing sugar and whisk again. Set in the fridge to cool for an hour.

Slice up the strawberries.

I serve this dessert in cocktail glasses or just glasses.

Pour the beautiful mascarpone into you welcome receptacles and dress with the sliced strawberries.

Drizzle over the maraschino.

SPOLIA OPTIMA
How Sweet it is

This phrase means that the best spoils are taken by a victorious army.

APRICOT AND ALMOND CAKE WITH WHIPPED VANILLA CREAM

The Ingredients

Four ounces of dried apricots (or tinned, if that is easier)

Eight ounces of butter

Three eggs

Eight ounces of caster sugar

Three ounces of ground almonds

Three ounces of plain flour

The juice of one lemon

Double cream

Preparation Time: 15 minutes
Cooking Time: 40 minutes
Serves: 4 – 6 but be quick !

Albicocca e Torta con Crema

*

PERSICUM ET AMYGDALINUS ET CRUSTULAM CRÈME

Preheat oven to 180°. Lightly butter your cake tin.

Slice up the apricots and put in a blender for a few minutes.

Mix up the butter and caster sugar and give them a through beating.

Whisk up the eggs and add to the butter and sugar with the almonds and lemon juice. Then fold in the flour and apricots.

Put in your cake tin and bake for about 30 – 35 minutes.

Let your cake breathe for two minutes and then it is ready to serve with the whipped vanilla cream. Hot or cold it is quite delicious.

DULCIA DOMESTICA
Homemade cakes

LOVE ON THE ROCKS STRAWBERRIES IN A BUTTERSCOTCH FIZZ

The Ingredients

One pound of strawberries

Four ounces of soft brown sugar

Two ounces of butter

Two tablespoons of golden syrup

A vanilla pod

A generous glass of Prosecco
(you and your guests can drink the rest
of the bottle)

Whipping cream and pistachio nuts

Preparation Time: 10 minutes
Cooking Time: 7 minutes
Serves: 4

Ami Sulle Rocce Fragole e una Fizz Butterscotch

*

AMO FRAGA CUM BUTTERSCOTCH SCINTILLARE

First, make up the butterscotch fizz.

Heat up the butter and add the sugar and syrup together with the vanilla pod gently.

Simmer for 5 minutes. Meanwhile slice the strawberries and chill.

Mix in the whipping cream and the champagne.

Add in the strawberries and give your dessert a good swirl.

Top up your triumph with pistachio nuts.

And straight to the table…

AMOR AB IMO PECTORE
Love from the heart

PEACHES IN A GOLDEN SYRUP AND PISTACHIO NUT POSSET

The Ingredients

Four peaches – fresh or tinned

Two ounces of golden syrup

One ounce of butter

Two ounces of soft brown sugar

One vanilla pod

One ounce of shelled pistachio nuts

Double cream

Preparation Time: 10 minutes
Cooking Time: 10 minutes
Serves: 4

Pesche in Scriroppe d'oro e Pistachio Nust Posset

*

PERSICA AUREUM SURREPO POSSET NUX

Peel the peaches and remove the stones or if they are tinned, you won't need to – you can happily cheat. I do it all the time.

Simmer on a very low heat in the golden syrup, butter, brown sugar with the vanilla pod for 5 minutes until delicately cooked and golden and still retaining their shape.

Plate up and swirl with the double cream and top with the pistachio nuts.

UNUS TIBI RESTAT NODUS
You have only one more nut to crack – but a hard one

Chapter Six
The Libations

RED WHITE AND BEAUTIFUL
MARASCHINO AND PROSECCO
COCKTAILS

The Liquid Infusions

A quarter of a pint of maraschino

A bottle of Prosecco

Galliano – just a few tablespoons

Raspberries to float on top and some cracked ice

Rosso Bianco e Bella Maraschino et Prosecco

*

ALBUM ET RUFUS ET PULCHER MARASCHINO LIBAMENTUM

Mix the above ingredients in a cocktail shaker.

Shake well.

Put in a serving jug and then set the raspberries for decoration atop.

The colour is glorious and the cocktails taste divine.

Perfect for a pre-prandial drink.

HOC TUUM EST OFFICIUM PULCRAM
It's your duty to be beautiful

HOME-MADE LEMONADE WITH A VODKA KICK

The Ingredients

Six lemons

Six ounces of granulated sugar

Two pints of boiling water

Half a pint of vodka

Preparation Time: 10 minutes
Resting Time: Overnight in a cool place
Serves: As many as everyone can drink until it runs out – which it will swiftly…

There is nothing quite like home-made lemonade – ice cold in Roma.

Pare the lemon zest with a zester or if you don't have one – but they are worth the investment – if not use a sharp knife.

Put the zest into a glass bowl and follow with the squeezed lemons juice.

Add the two pints of boiling water and the sugar, then store in bottles in a cool place overnight and before so – give your limonella a good stir from time to time.

Again keep ice cold until ready to serve.

Children love it and will obviously have it pure but for those more adventurous adults, tip in some vodka. A slice of lemon on top.

Chill your cocktail glasses and dip in a small bowl of caster sugar to give it a heavenly halo. Then pour in the lemonade and serve up.

ALTISSIMA QUAEQUE FLUMINA MINOMO SONO LABI
Still waters run deep

Well, to give you an explanation, this is a Roman Proverb meaning not to reduce those who strive for self-promotion but at the same time advising not to blow one's own trumpet.

TAKE YOUR BREATH AWAY
SEA BREEZE

The Ingredients

Quarter of a bottle of Blue Curaçao

Four tablespoons of pineapple juice

A bottle of champagne

A goodly dash of grenadine

Pineapple wedge for the decoration on top

Crushed ice

Preparation Time: 5 minutes
Serves: Whoever gets there first

Togliere il Fiato Brezza Marina

*

MARE AUFERET VENTUS TOLLET SPIRITUM

Place the Curaçao, pineapple juice and not forgetting the champagne in a cocktail shaker and then, well, give it all a few good shakes.

Lace in the grenadine and add the ice.

The cocktail will be a heady and brilliant blue colour. Difficult to resist......

Top up your glasses with the pineapple wedges and distribute to your willing guests.

TERRA MARITIMUS
Beyond the sea

ANGEL'S SNIFTER

The Volatile Infusions

Half a pint of watermelon juice

Half a pint of gin

Lots of crushed ice

Slim watermelon slices to garnish

Add a little shredded mint

Brandi di Angel

*

ANGELUS SCRIPTOR

Combine the watermelon juice and the gin in a cocktail shaker.

Give it a good shake and add the crushed ice.

Pour into you pristine glasses and garnish with the watermelon slices and shredded mint.

This is a very simple cocktail, audacious and refreshing.

QUANDO ROMAE SUM IEIUNO SABBATO
When in Rome do as the Romans do

The background to this historical adage is
'When I am in Rome, I fast on a Saturday'
Which means – follow local traditions out of respect.

EXTRAORDINARY SPICED WINE

The Flammable Infusions

One and a half pints of red wine

Two Sticks of vanilla pod

Four Tablespoons of honey

I shredded pomegranate

One teaspoon of saffron

The juice and zest of one lemon and one teaspoon of grated nutmeg

Vino Spezie Straordinaria

*

CONDITUM PARADOXUM

Firstly, melt the honey on a low heat for a few minutes and then drench in half a bottle of red wine.

Cook for a few moments, then add the vanilla pods, pomegranate, nutmeg and saffron.

Finally add the lemon and the rest of the wine.

Sieve before you serve to release the pomegranate seeds but the fruit does give the spiced wine a lovely rosy glow so worth the effort.

Warm up and serve hot.

It is a perfect libation on a chilly winter's afternoon or evening.

And as Martial said in his Epigrams 12.12:
"When you drink into the night Pollio,
you promise me everything
But in the morning you offer me nothing.
So Pollio, drink in the morning."

SOME LIKE IT HOT IN THE SUMMERTIME ORCHARD CUP

The Ingredients

Four bottles of Italian dry wine

And a bottle of sparkling wine

One cup of Calvados

One bottle of apple juice

Two apples

The juice of one lemon

Apple blossom for decoration

Preparation Time: 15 minutes
Then leave to chill for: 30 minutes
Serves: Lots of happy guests

Pour the wine, sparkling wine and Calvados into a punch bowl and then add the apple juice.

Put in the fridge and whilst this heavenly drink is chilling, core and slice up the apples and sit in some lemon juice in order to prevent any discolouration.

And then just lift out and float the apple on top of your punch bowl.

If it is the right time of year, bedeck with apple blossom.

SOL LUCET OMNIBUS
The sun shines for everyone

THE LAST WORD GOES TO
THE VENERABLE DORMOUSE

A delicacy in Classical times
And he was a regular guest at banquets.
My research tells me they humanely despatched
The dormice to the Underworld but as I was not
around over two thousand years ago
I did not witness and cannot attest to this but
I hope this is the truth.
Wrapped in parma ham and showered with
poppy seeds and honey
was one favoured recipe.
Of course you don't want to indulge in this
culinary expedition and nor do I
But I thought it was an interesting, ancient fact
And part of Classical culture.
Glis glis are a protected species nowadays
so they can sleep safe.
As a special tribute to all dormice
and to end the book …

'The Dormouse lay happy, his eyes were so tight,
He could see no chrysanthemums, yellow or white
And all that he felt at the back of his head
Were delphiniums blue and geraniums red"

When We Were Young (A.A. Milne, 1924)

Hail Dormouse – Vale Glis

The End